A Collection
Of
Latin Maxims
And Phrases
Literally Translated

by

John N. Cotterell

A Collection Of Latin Maxims And Phrases Literally Translated by John N. Cotterell

ISBN: 978-93-58012-15-6

Published by

DOUBLE 9 BOOKS

2/13-B, Ansari Road
Daryaganj, New Delhi – 110002
info@double9books.com
www.double9books.com
Tel. 011-40042856

ABOUT THE AUTHOR

John N. Cotterell was a novelist who worked on a book with his amazing thoughts, which resulted in A Collection Of Latin Maxims And Phrases Literally translated. This collection of Latin expressions with their English translation written by John N. Cotterell attempts to compile many of his classic thoughts and offer them at an affordable price, in an attractive volume so that everyone can read them. This book by John N. Cotterell aims to help readers understand and use Latin phrases in everyday language, particularly in legal, academic, and philosophical contexts.

CONTENTS

PREFACE TO FIRST EDITION.

The Author, from the commencement of his study of the law, and more especially during his course of reading for the intermediate and final examinations, became convinced of the very great advantage to be reaped from a knowledge of the leading Latin Maxims, now so frequently quoted in all legal works; those given hereafter will be found to comprise all that occur in the recognised examination text-books, having been collected from such works.

It will be remembered that a maxim is a general principle and universally approved leading truth; therefore, even the most elementary student cannot do better than store away in his memory some of the more important of these rules as a foundation for future study. At every law examination questions are to be found that bear directly on some one or other of the principles contained in these maxims, and they are often quoted, the student being required to translate and explain their meaning and application—they are, in fact, equally important with Leading Cases.

Those maxims only have been selected which are constantly met with by the student, and which he would do well to commit to memory; leading cases are also referred to. The explanations have been made as brief as possible, and for deeper research the student is referred to Broom's Legal Maxims.

Walsall, 1881.

PREFACE TO SECOND AND THIRD EDITIONS.

After a busy and practical experience of many years the writer can now in all earnestness—as during the days of studentship he did in all distrust and doubtfulness—emulate the writer of old who said—

"Cognitio legis est copulata et complicata."

Our greatest writers of more recent years have also recognised the intricate and ever-changing study of the Law. The late Lord Tennyson, in that most beautiful poem, "Aylmer's Field," tells us—

"So Leolin went; and as we task ourselves

To learn a language known but smatteringly

In phrases here and there at random—toiled

Mastering the lawless science of our law,

That codeless myriad of precedent,

That wilderness of single instances,

Thro' which a few, by wit or fortune led,

May beat a pathway out to wealth and fame."

Those who wish to follow successfully the law as a profession must remain students to the last, and the leading truths and time-honoured legal principles, as defined by the maxims hereafter contained, will ever serve alike as safe landmarks, and sheet anchors, in times of doubt and uncertainty.

Since the publication of the First Edition, the number of maxims (very properly defined as the condensed good sense of nations) has been considerably enlarged, but the student will find the more important ones prefixed by an asterisk, and these may with advantage be memorized.

Walsall, 1913.

A COLLECTION OF LATIN MAXIMS AND PHRASES.

*** 1. A verbis legis non recedendum est.** *The words of the law must not be departed from.*

Acts of Parliament must be interpreted strictly according to the express letters of their respective clauses. Although in certain cases an equitable construction can be placed on the words, yet this principle is confined within certain limits; and a judge cannot, in favour of a presumable intention, depart from such words when, for anything that appears, the wording may correspond with the design of the legislature. (See Steph. Comm.)

*** 2. Accessorium non ducit sed sequitur suum principale.** *The accessory does not lead but follows its principal.*

The grant of a reversion will also include a rent incident thereto—so heir-looms follow the inheritance.

3. Accusare nemo se debet, nisi coram Deo. *No one is in duty bound to accuse himself unless before God.*

In certain cases a witness is not compelled to answer, if by so doing he would incriminate himself. (See Max. No. 171.)

*** 4. Acta exteriora indicant interiora secreta.** *Overt acts make known latent thoughts,* or *Acts indicate the intention.*

Where an authority given by law is abused, the person becomes a trespasser *ab initio*, but not so if authority be given by party, or in cases of mere non-feasance. (*Six Carpenters' Case*, 1 Smith, L. C. 11th ed.)

*** 5. Actio personalis moritur cum personâ.** *A personal action dies with the person.*

In actions of tort this was formerly a general rule, but recently its application has been so generally narrowed that it probably affects only actions for libel and slander. By Lord Campbell's Act, 9 & 10 Vict. c. 93, compensation may, however, now be recovered by the relatives of a person negligently killed. Compensation may also be recovered in some cases of trespass. (See Chitty, 16th ed.)

6. Actus curiae neminem gravabit. *The act of the Court shall prejudice no man.*

(*Cumber v. Wane*, 1 Sm. L. C. 11th ed.)

*** 7. Actus Dei nemini facit injuriam.** *The act of God causes injury to no one.*

Storms, tempests, and the like, are acts of God, being inevitable accidents not caused by man.

8. Actus me invito, non est meus actus. *An involuntary act is not one's own act, i.e., an act done against one's will is not such person's act.*

The law presumes coercion in certain cases—by a husband over his wife. Intentions denominate the action, and especially so in criminal cases. (See next Max. and Nos. 116 and 285.)

*** 9. Actus non facit reum, nisi mens sit rea.** *The act itself does not make a man guilty, unless his intention be so.*

There must be a vicious will or criminal intention as well as an unlawful act. (See Maxs. Nos. 8, 116 and 285.) Where one engaged in doing a lawful act, without any wrongful intention, unfortunately and inadvertently kills another person, the homicide is excusable.

10. Ad questiones facti non respondent judices; ad questiones legis non respondent juratores. *Judges do not decide questions of fact; the jury do not decide questions of law.*

This applies to trials by jury, and where the issue turns rather upon facts than legal construction, such method of trial is usually, but not necessarily, followed.

*** 11. Aequitas factum habet quod fieri oportuit.** *Equity looks upon that as done which ought to have been done.*

The doctrine of satisfaction well illustrates this principle of law. (See Max. No. 74.) Where a person is under an obligation to perform an act, equity looks on it as done, and allows the same results to follow as if it were actually done. Thus, when one who has contracted to sell realty dies, the purchase money therefor forms part of his estate, and goes to his next of kin, if intestate, such realty being deemed in equity to be vested in the contractee. (See *Fletcher v. Ashburner*, 1 Wh. & Tu. 8th ed.)

12. Aequitas nunquam contravenit leges. *Equity never opposes the law.*

To supplement, and not to contravene, is its object.

*** 13. Aequitas sequitur legem.** *Equity follows the law. Equity cannot alter the law of the land, but follows it.*

Both in the sense of obeying the law, and conforming to its general rules and policy, and also in applying to equitable estates and interests the rules by which at common law legal estates and interests of a similar kind are governed.

14. Agentes et consentientes pari poenâ plectentur. *Acting and consenting parties are liable to the same punishment.*

A person aiding and abetting the actual commission of a crime, either at the scene of its commission or elsewhere, is equally liable with the perpetrator, the former being a principal in the second degree, and the latter in the first degree. If A., with intent to murder, inflicts on B. an injury dangerous to life, aided and abetted by C., who is aware of the intent, they are both equally guilty and punishable.

*** 15. Alienatio rei praefertur juri accrescendi.** *The law favours alienation rather than accumulation.*

This maxim has always been the policy of our law, even from the time when the right of subinfeudation was first recognised. The statutes of *De Donis*, 13 Edw. I. c. 1 and *Quia emptores*, 18 Edw. I. c. 1, are examples in proof of this doctrine. Also the rules against perpetuities, which forbid any executory interests to take effect later than a life or lives in being or twenty-one years afterwards, allowance being made for gestation where the same actually exists.

16. Allegans contraria non est audiendus. *One who contradicts himself is not to be heard.*

A rule of evidence relative to the credibility of a witness. Cross-examination is frequently used to this end.

17. Allegans suam turpitudinem non est audiendus. *A person boasting of his own wrong-doing is not to be heard.*

When a person does an act which may be rightfully performed, he cannot say that such act was intentionally done wrongly. See *In re Hallett, Knatchbull v. Hallett*, 13 Ch. Div. 696, where an *obiter dictum* found in the judgment of the Court is as follows: "When we come to apply that principle" (*i.e.*, the one given above) "to the case of a trustee who has blended trust moneys with his own, it seems perfectly plain that he cannot be heard to say that he took away the trust money, when he had a right to take away his own money."

*** 18. Ambiguitas contra stipulatorem est.** *An ambiguity is taken against the party using it.*

Thus, if in a lease, words of exception be used ambiguously, the same being words of the lessor, are construed most strongly as against him. (See Chitty on Contracts, 16th ed.; also Max. No. 272.)

*** 19. Ambiguitas verborum latens verificatione suppletur;
nam quod ex facto oritur ambiguum verificatione facti
tollitur.** *A hidden ambiguity of the words may be interpreted by
evidence; for an ambiguity which arises from an extrinsic fact may
be removed by proof of such fact.*

(See Max. No. 20.)

*** 20. Ambiguitas verborum patens nullâ verificatione
excluditur.** *A patent ambiguity of the words cannot be removed by
extrinsic evidence.*

The last two maxims are most important in the construction of contracts.
Thus upon a devise, "to one of the sons of J. S.," who has several sons, parol
evidence would not be admissible to ascertain which son in particular was
referred to. (Max. No. 19.) But where there is a devise of "the Manor of A.," the
testator having two estates of that description, this being a latent ambiguity,
parol evidence is admissible to explain which was meant.

21. Amicus curie. *A friend to the Court,* i.e., *one who advises
disinterestedly and spontaneously.*

22. Aqua cedit solo. *Water passes with the soil.*

From a legal point of view, water is land covered by water, and an action
cannot be brought to recover possession of a pool, &c., by the name of water
only, but as so much land covered by water. Water, being a movable thing,
must continue common, and its ownership therefore goes with the land below.

Where a river divides the property of two different persons, the bed of
the river is equally divided between them; and, according to Bracton, if an
island rise in midstream, it belongs in common to those possessing land on
each side thereof, but if it be nearer to one bank than the other, it belongs to
the proprietor of the nearer shore. (See Steph. Comm. Vol. I. 15th ed. Cap. 1.)

23. Aqua currit et debet currere. *Water flows and should be
allowed to flow.*

No one can have any right of property in a running stream, but only a
right to use it; and this must be so exercised as not to interfere with other
persons possessing similar rights.

24. Auctori incumbit onus probandi. *The onus of proof lies on
the plaintiff.*

(See Maxs. Nos. 69 and 252.)

25. Audi alteram partem. *Hear the other side* (i.e., *Do not
condemn a man unheard.*)

This is one of the fundamental principles of the British Constitution.

*** 26. Benignae faciendae sunt interpretationes chartarum, ut
res magis valeat quam pereat.** *Constructions of documents are
to be made favourably, that the instrument may rather avail than
perish.*

See hereon *Roe* v. *Tranmarr*, 2 Sm. L. C. 556, which is a most important case for reference with regard to the construction and interpretation of written instruments. The facts as quoted from Smith were as follows. "A., in consideration of natural love, and of £100, by deeds of lease and release *granted*, released, and confirmed certain premises *after his own death*, to his brother, B., in tail, remainder to C. (the son of another brother of A.) in fee; and he covenanted and granted that the premises should after his death be held by B. and the heirs of his body, or by C. and his heirs, according to the true intent of the deed. Held, that the deed could not operate as a release, because it attempted to convey a freehold in futuro, but that it was good as a covenant to stand seised." Want of technical knowledge on the part of contracting parties must be allowed for. Words should be subservient to the intention, if this can be gathered from the instrument itself. (See Maxs. Nos. 211, 236, 250, 273, and 275.)

27. Bis dat qui cito dat. *He gives twice who gives quickly.*

*** 28. Caveat emptor (Qui ignorare non debuit quod jus alienum emit).**
Let the buyer beware (who ought not to be ignorant what he buys from another).

The law implies no warranty of goodness or quality on sale of goods, and the maxim applies in such cases, it being remembered that "Simplex commendatio non obligat." (See Max. No. 255.) If goods be ordered for any particular purpose, or of a particular description, or if the purchaser has had no opportunity of judging for himself, the maxim would not apply, as in such cases warranty is implied.—Nor in cases where there is "suppressio veri" or "suggestio falsi" on the part of the vendor. And see hereon *Brown* v. *Eddington*, 2 Scott, N. R. 504; and Chitty on Contracts, 16th ed.

29. Cessante ratione legis, cessat ipsa lex. *The reason of the law
being at an end, the law itself ceases.*

Reason is always the acknowledged soul of the law.

**30. Chirographum apud debitorem repertum praesumitur
solutum.** *A deed found with a debtor is presumed to be satisfied.*

If a person, who has effected a mortgage on his property, again gets the deeds into his possession, it is presumed that the loan has been repaid, even though no reconveyance has been taken.

*** 31. Clausulae inconsuetae semper inducunt suspicionem.**
Unusual clauses always excite suspicion.

In *Twyne's Case* (1 Sm. L. C. 11th ed.), a deed containing a clause that the gift was made "honestly, truly, and bonâ fide," was held fraudulent and void, even although made for valuable consideration. (See Maxs. Nos. 61 and 63.) The French maxim of "Qui s'excuse s'accuse" may in like cases be noted with advantage.

32. Cognovit actionem. *He had admitted the action.*

33. Commodum ex injuriâ suâ nemo habere debet. *No one should have an advantage from his own wrong.*

34. Conditio sine qua non. *A condition without which the matter cannot be.*

35. Consensus tollit errorem. *Consent removes a mistake*; or, as Broom says, *"the acquiescence of a party who might take advantage of an error, obviates its effect."*

The doctrine of waiver is referable to this maxim (See also Maxs. Nos. 216, 217 and 222.)

36. Constructio legis, non fecit injuriam. *Construction of the law causes no injury.*

*** 37. Consuetudo ex certâ causa rationabili usitata privat communem legem.** *A custom based on a certain reasonable foundation obrogates the common law.*

For example may be cited the custom of gavelkind, under which the land of a deceased person descended to all his sons equally, and the custom of Borough English, under which it descended alone to the youngest son. Both these customs supersede the common law of descent. (See Steph. Comm., Vol. I., and Maxs. Nos. 38, 153 and 197.)

38. Consuetudo pro lege servatur. *Custom is protected by the law.*

(See also Max. No. 37.)

39. Contemporanea exposito est optima et fortissima in lege. *A contemporaneous interpretation is the best and strongest in law.*

In interpreting an old document or statute, consideration must be had for the intention and intended effect at the time of its execution, on the ground that the same were then best known and appreciated. (See Chitty on Contracts, 16th ed. and Max. No. 275.)

*** 40. Contra non valentem agere nulla currit praescriptio.** *No prescription runs against one unable to act.*

Generally, prescription runs only from the time when the plaintiff might have brought his action, unless then under disability. In actions brought to recover land, rent, or legacies, a certain additional time is allowed after the disability ceases. In actions having reference only to things strictly personal, the same time is allowed after the disability ceases, as would have been allowed at the time the cause of action accrued had no such disability then existed.

*** 41. Contractus ex turpi causa, vel contra bonos mores, nullus.** *A contract arising from a base consideration, or against morality, is void.*

A contract made in consideration of past seduction is not binding. (*Beaumont* v. *Reeve*, 8 Q. B. 483.) Also a betting or wagering contract.

*** 42. Cuicunque aliquid conceditur, conceditur et id sine quo res ipsa esse non potuit.** *To whomsoever anything is conceded, that also is given, without which the thing itself cannot be.*

(See Max. No. 210.)

43. Cuilibet in sua arte perito est credendum. *Each one skilled in his own art is to be believed.*

Medical men and other skilled witnesses, may give their opinion in evidence, as to the state or condition of a patient or thing at any particular time. Expert evidence is always admissible, but being expensive and not conclusive, is weighed cautiously and little relied upon.

(See Max. No. 226.)

44. Cujus est dare, ejus est disponere. *Whose it is to give, his it is to dispose;* or, as Broom says, *"The bestower of a gift has a right to regulate its disposal."*

This rule is a general one, but considerably curtailed and qualified at the present time, especially so by the Acts which restrict and regulate the tying up of Real Estate, and accumulation of personal property beyond specified periods.

45. Cujus est divisio, alterius est electio. *When one divides, the other has the right of first choice.*

In the case of an estate being held in coparcenary, partition thereof was formerly sometimes made voluntarily, by the eldest parcener dividing, in which case she chose last. But by Statute 8 & 9 Vic. c. 106, s. 3, all partitions must now be by deed in order to be binding. (See Steph. Comm. Vol. I.)

46. Cujus est solum, ejus est usque ad coelum et ad inferos. *Whose is the soil, his it is even to the skies and to the depths below.*

Upon a conveyance of land, *simpliciter,* buildings, and timber being thereon will also pass, as also the mines thereunder, — "donec probeter in contrarium" (*i.e.,* until the contrary is proved). Property, however, must be so used and enjoyed as not to injure or prejudice the rights of adjoining owners, as by overhanging buildings. (See Max. No. 254.) This maxim affords an illustration of the rule that the word land is *nomen generalissimum*—a most general term. (See Maxs. Nos. 188 and 224.)

47. Culpa lata dolo aequiparatur. *Gross negligence is equivalent to intentional wrong.*

(See Max. No. 223.)

48. Cum confitente sponte, mitius est agendum. *He who willingly confesses, should be dealt with more leniently.*

Confession to a crime, when committed, always operates in mitigation of punishment. Penitence for wrong-doing should not be allowed to go unrecognised.

*** 49. Cum duo inter se pugnantia reperiuntur in testamento ultimum ratum est.** *Where two repugnant clauses (or statements) occur in a will, the latter shall prevail.*

It will be remembered, however, that the intention must in all cases be looked to and if possible carried out, and the above maxim is a rule only inasmuch as its application generally will do this. Moreover, it has no reference to deeds, where, if there be two such repugnant clauses, the first is received and the latter rejected. (See Maxs. Nos. 78 and 275.)

50. Curia advisare vult. *The court desires to consider.*

In difficult cases judgment is frequently reserved.

51. De fide et officio juridicis non recipitur quaestio, sed de scientia sive sit error juris sive facti. *The decision of a judge may be impugned only for error either in law or of fact, but his honesty of purpose or office cannot be questioned.*

*** 52. De minimis non curat lex.** *The law cares not about mere trifles.*

Where the ocean gradually recedes, or washes up sand and earth, and thus in time forms *terra firma*, the land so resulting belongs to the owner of that immediately behind and adjoining; if, however, the dereliction or alluvion be sudden, the land thus formed belongs to the Crown. (See *Westbury-on-Severn Rural Sanitary Authority* v. *Meredith*, 30 Ch. Div. 387.)

53. Debita sequuntur personam debitoris. *Debts follow the debtor's person.*

*** 54. Debitor non praesumitur donare.** *A debtor is not presumed to give.*

This maxim has reference to the law of satisfaction. Where a debtor bequeaths to his creditor a sum of money equal to, or exceeding the amount of his debt, it is presumed, in the absence of any contrary intention, that such legacy was meant and given by the testator as a satisfaction of the debt. (See *Talbot* v. *Shrewsbury*, 2 Wh. & Tu. 8th ed.) This presumption of satisfaction, however, does not arise where the debt was not contracted until after the will was made, or where it was secured by a Bill of Exchange or other negotiable instrument, or where the legacy was contingent, not payable immediately on testator's death, or of a specific chattel. (See Snell's Equity, 16th ed.; also Max. No. 56.)

*** 55. Delegatus non potest delegare.** *An agent cannot delegate his authority.*

A principal (except by his own assent) is not bound by the acts or contracts of subagents unless they be of necessity, or in accordance with the usual custom of trade. *Delegata potestas non potest delegari.* (See Chitty on Contracts, 16th ed.; and Maxs. Nos. 194, 208, and 280.)

56. Delicatus debitor est odiosus in lege. *An extravagant debtor is contemned in the eye of the law.*

By the Bankruptcy Act, 1883, the Court may either refuse a bankrupt his discharge, or suspend its operation, on proof that he has brought on his bankruptcy by an unjustifiable extravagance in living. (See Max. No. 54.)

57. Dentur omnes decimae primariae ecclesiae ad quam parochia pertinet. *All tithes must be paid to the Mother Church to which the parish belongs.*

This was a law of King Edgar, prior to which every man paid his tithe to whatever church or parish he thought fit. (See Steph. Comm. 15th ed. Vol. I.)

58. Descendit jus quasi ponderosum quid, cadens deorsum recta linea; et nunquam reascendit ea via qua descendit. *The right of inheritance descends like a heavy body, falling in a straight line; and it never ascends by the same line that it came down.*

This was one of the old laws of descent, under which the lineal ancestor himself was always excluded, although his issue, being the collateral heirs of the deceased, might inherit the latter's land. Now, however, by the Inheritance Act, 1833, 3 & 4 Will. IV. c. 106, on failure of the issue of the purchaser, the inheritance descends to the nearest lineal ancestor in the preferable line, provided that no issue of a nearer deceased ancestor in that line exists. (See Steph. Comm. Vol. I. *et seq.*, and Max. No. 102.)

59. Deus solus haeredem facere potest, non homo. *God alone is able to make an heir and not man.*

(See Max. No. 165.)

60. Dies Dominicus non est juridicus. *Sunday is not a day for judicial proceedings.*

61. Dolosus versatur in generalibus. *A deceiver deals in generalities*—i.e., *uses ambiguous terms.*

One of the reasons for the decision in *Twine's Case*, 1 Sm. L. C. 11th ed., was "That the gift had the signs and marks of fraud, because it was general, without exception even of his apparel or anything of necessity, for it is commonly said *'quod dolosus versatur in generalibus.'*" (See Maxs. Nos. 31 and 63.)

*** 62. Domus sua cuique est tutissimum refugium.** *To every man his own house is the safest refuge*—i.e., *Every man's house is his castle*—"Nemo de domo sua extrahi potest."

It has been decided, however, that the sheriff may lawfully break into the house of a defendant in the following cases:—where the house is recovered by any real action, or by ejectment in pursuance of the writ "*habere facias possessionem,*" also where the king is a party. The house of one man is a privilege or castle for himself only, and not for one who flies to him for protection. (*Semayne's Case*, 1 Sm. L. C. 121. See Max. 162.)

63. Dona clandestina sunt semper suspiciosa. *Clandestine gifts are always suspicious.*

The gift in *Twyne's Case*, 1 Sm. L. C. 11th ed., was made in secret. (See Maxs. Nos. 31 and 61.)

64. Donatio non praesumitur. *A gift is not presumed.*

The law with reference to gifts is most stringent, and strict proof is usually required.

*** 65. Donationes sint stricti juris, ne quis plus donasse praesumatur quam in donatione expressit.** *Gifts are to be construed strictly according to law, lest any one be presumed to have given more than he may actually have set forth in the gift or grant.*

See *Stat. De Donis Conditionalibus*, 13 Ed. I. c. 1, which by its enactments laid the foundation of our present Estates Tail.

The word "heirs" was formerly necessary in order to create by deed an estate in fee simple, or in tail; if land were given to a man for ever, or to him and his assigns for ever, he would take only an estate for life. By the Conveyancing Act the use of the word "heirs" is no longer necessary, the words "in fee simple," or "in fee tail," being sufficient, as the case may be.

66. Duces tecum. *You must bring with you.*

A form of subpœna when production of documents is required.

67. Duo non possunt in solido unam rem possidere. *Two cannot possess the whole of one thing in its entirety.*

68. Ea quae raro accidunt, non temere in agendis negotiis computantur. *Such things as seldom occur, are not rashly to be taken into account in business transactions.*

*** 69. Ei incumbit probatio qui affirmat, non qui negat; cum per rerum naturam factum negantis probatio nulla sit.** *He must prove a thing who says it, not he who denies it, since by the nature of things he who denies a fact cannot produce any proof; i.e., the proof lies upon him who affirms, and not upon him who denies.*

It is a general rule that in the trial of all actions the plaintiff should begin. (See Maxs. Nos. 24 and 252.)

* 70. Equality is Equity.

Persons making purchases for a joint undertaking are held tenants in common in equity, although at law they are joint tenants. (See *Lake* v. *Gibson* and *Lake* v. *Craddock*, 2 Wh. and Tud. L. C. Eq. 8th ed. 973.) Equity, where possible, always favours a tenancy in common as opposed to a joint tenancy.

* 71. Equity acts in personam: i.e., *against the person.*

Judgments of Courts of Law were always enforced *in rem*, by writ of *fieri facias*, &c., but the decrees of the Court of Chancery could always be enforced *in personam*, by attachment. (See *Penn* v. *Lord Baltimore*, 1 Wh. and Tud. L. C. 8th ed.)

*** 72. Equity imputes an intention to fulfil an obligation.** (*If the thing actually done might have been done with an intention to fulfil an obligation.*)

The equitable doctrines of satisfaction (see *Talbot* v. *Duke of Shrewsbury* and *Chancey's Case*, 2 Wh. & Tud. L. C. Eq. 8th ed.) and performance (see *Wilcocks* v. *Wilcocks*, and *Blandy* v. *Widmore*, 2 Wh. and Tud. L. C. Eq. 8th ed.), have recourse to this maxim, and the principle upon which they are founded is the one therein contained.

73. Equity never wants a trustee.

Where a valid trust exists, equity will impose on the person in whom the legal estate is vested the duty and obligation of carrying out such trust.

* 74. Equity regards the spirit and not the letter.

Equity looks at the intention of the parties, and not at the actual words employed in any transaction. Equity always regarded a mortgage as an instrument to secure the repayment of money, and allowed the mortgagor to redeem at any time, but at Common Law, unless the mortgagor paid back the money by the day named in the mortgage deed, his right of redemption was gone. (See Maxs. Nos. 11 and 196.)

> **75. Erant omnia communia et indivisa omnibus, veluti unum cunctis patrimonium esset.** *All things were common and undivided to all people, as if there were one property for all.*

See Justin I. 43, c. 1. While there were yet few inhabitants on the face of the globe, it seems probable and reasonable that all things were in common among them, and that each took from the public stock what he might require for immediate purposes, and that the right of possession was coexistent only with actual possession. (See Steph. Comm. Vol. I. Book II.)

> **76. Esse optime constitutam rempublican, quae ex tribus generibus illis, regali** (*monarchy*), **optimo** (*aristocracy*), **et populari** (*democracy*), **sit modice confusa.** *That State is the best constituted which is made up in moderation of the three classes, royalty, nobility, and commons.*

The truth of this is generally admitted—our own country, which comprises the three above essentials, being universally acknowledged the best governed kingdom in the world.

> **77. Est boni judicis ampliare jurisdictionem (et justitiam).** *It is the duty of a good judge to enlarge his jurisdiction and also justice itself; i.e., to extend the remedies of the law, and without usurping jurisdiction, to apply its rules to the advancement of justice.*

Where a case comes before a court of law, in which it has hitherto been the practice to refuse relief to the plaintiff or defendant, as the case may be, and consequently to drive such party to seek redress in the Court of Chancery, it is expedient for all parties and the public at large, that such court of law, and its judge, should act in a liberal and uncramped manner, and if possible apply the necessary remedy. (See *Collins* v. *Blantern*, 1 Smith, L. C. 11th ed.) By the Judicature Acts, "law" and "equity" are to be concurrently administered in all Courts, but the true spirit of this maxim must ever stand good.

> *** 78. Ex antecedentibus et consequentibus fit optima interpretatio.** *From what goes before and what follows, the best interpretation is arrived at.*

The context must be most thoroughly looked into before a correct interpretation can be obtained. This maxim is one of the most important rules for the construction of contracts, which in all cases are to be favourably construed according to their object, and the whole of their terms. (See Chitty on Contracts, 16th ed. and Maxs. Nos. 26, 177, 214 and 272.)

79. Ex diuturnitate temporis omnia praesumuntur rite esse acta. *After a length of time all things are presumed to have been properly done.*

The Prescription Act, 2 & 3 Will. IV. c. 71, is in point upon this maxim.

*** 80. Ex dolo malo non oritur actio.** *An action does not arise from a fraud.*

(See Maxs. Nos. 82, 182 and 234.)

*** 81. Ex nudo pacto non oritur actio.** *An action does not arise from a nude contract.*

Every simple contract must be supported by a valuable consideration, as money, marriage, or the like. A good consideration (*i.e.,* relationship, or natural love and affection) will not support an assumpsit. Chitty lays down the rule "that a sufficient consideration or recompense for making, or motive or inducement to make, the promise upon which a party is charged, is of the very essence of a contract not under seal, both at law and in equity; and that such consideration must exist, or the promise will be void and no action be maintainable thereon." Such consideration may be either executed, executory, concurrent or continuing.

*** 82. Ex turpi causâ non oritur actio.** *No action arises from an immoral cause (or base consideration).*

Contracts founded on a consideration which is *contra bonos mores* are void. See also *Merryweather* v. *Nixan,* 2 Smith, L. C. 398, where it was decided that there is no right of contribution between joint tort-feasors. (See Maxs. Nos. 80, 182 and 232.)

83. Exceptio probat regulam. *Exception proves the rule.*

(See Max. No. 174.)

84. Executio juris non habet injuriam. *The execution of the law works no injury.* **Actus legis neminem est damnosum.** *The act of the law is hurtful to none.*

*** 85. Expressio coram quae tacitè insunt, nihil operatur.** *The express mention of those things which are tacitly implied, has no effect.*

A voluntary courtesy is insufficient to support a subsequent promise, unless there has been an antecedent request, and such request must be proved at the trial, except where the consideration, though executed, is of such a nature that it must necessarily have been moved by a previous request, and in which case therefore, such a statement becomes merely "expressio eorum quae tacitè insunt," and is consequently unnecessary. (*Lampleigh* v. *Braithwait,* 1 Smith, L. C. 11th ed.)

86. Expressio unius est exclusio alterius. *The express mention of one thing causes the exclusion of another.*

Where in a mortgage of several properties the following general words were used, "together with all grates, boilers, &c., and other fixtures in and about the said two dwelling-houses and the brewhouse thereunto belonging," it was ruled that the fixtures in the other mortgaged property did not pass to the mortgagee, although without these words they would have done. By particularising one or more members of a class, an intention may be inferred to exclude the rest.

*** 87. Expressum facit cessare tacitum.** *What is expressed makes what is implied to cease.*

The word "demise" in a lease implies a covenant for quiet enjoyment, but if such covenant be inserted, then the maxim will not apply. Implied contracts in law exist only where there is no express promise between the parties. (See Chitty on Contracts, 16th ed.)

*** 88. Falsa demonstratio non nocet.** *An erroneous description does not vitiate.*

Where in the former part of an instrument there is to be found a sufficiently clear and certain description, it will not be vitiated by a subsequent erroneous addition. (See Chitty on Contracts, 16th ed. and Maxs. Nos. 89 and 274.)

89. Falsa orthographia, sive falsa grammatica, non vitiat concessionem. *Incorrect spelling or ungrammatical expressions do not mar a gift.*

(See Maxs. Nos. 88 and 146.)

90. Falsus in uno falsus in omnibus. *False in one thing false in all.*

It will always be found best, "honeste vivere, alterum non laedere, sua cuique tribuere." Honesty is the best policy; once a knave always a knave.

91. Fatetur facinus qui judicium fugit. *He who flies from justice acknowledges himself a criminal.*

Under such circumstances the presumption is one of guilt.

*** 92. Fides est obligatio conscientiae alicujus ad intentionem alterius.** *A trust is the obligation of one's conscience to fulfil the intention of another.*

A trust is also defined as a beneficial interest in, or ownership of, real or personal property, unattended with the legal ownership thereof. (Snell's Eq. 16th ed. Part II.)

93. Fieri non debuit, sed factum valet. *It ought not to have been done, but having been done is valid.*

A marriage by persons under the age of twenty-one years without the consent of their father is valid, although by 4 Geo. IV. c. 76, s. 16, such consent is made requisite. (See Max. No. 228.)

94. Foreclose down, redeem up.

A mortgagee can only foreclose those claiming an interest in the mortgaged property after himself; but a mortgagor must redeem every mortgage, and any mortgagee, in order to obtain the rights of a first mortgagee, must redeem all mortgages prior to his own. (See Snell's Eq. 16th ed. Chap. XVI.)

95. Fractionem diei non recipit lex. *The law takes no note of a fraction of a day.*

When an act has to be done on a certain day, the whole of that day is allowed in which to do it. This rule has exceptions, however, for in case of documents registered on the same day, priority of registration may be shown by the numbers, and this becomes, at times, of the utmost importance.

96. Frater fratri sine legitimo haerede defuncto, in beneficio quod eorum patris fuit, succedat; sin autem unus e fratribus a domino feudum acceperit, eo defuncto sine legitimo haerede, frater ejus in feudum non succedit. *A brother may succeed a brother who has died without lawful heir in the benefice which belonged to their father; but if one brother shall have received a feud from a lord, if he dies without a lawful heir, his brother does not succeed to the feud.*

This is one of the old laws of inheritance, which are still of importance as leading to a perfect understanding of the Act of 1833. Formerly no one could succeed to an inheritance unless he was not only of the blood of the purchaser, but also his lineal issue, consequently one brother could not succeed to another brother's inheritance, of which the latter was the purchaser, because he could not be his brother's lineal issue, but where the inheritance had originally descended from an ancestor, one brother could succeed another, as he might be the lineal issue of such ancestor. (See Steph. Comm. I. 15th ed. *et seq.*, also next Maxim and No. 203.)

97. Frater fratri uterino non succedat in haereditate paternâ. *A brother shall not succeed a brother of the half blood in the father's estate.*

Another old law of inheritance, under which the half-blood were totally excluded, the land escheating to the lord of the manor rather than go to a kinsman bearing this relationship to the person from whom descent was to be traced. Now, however, since the Inheritance Act, s. 9, it is otherwise, the place in which any such relation by the half-blood stands in the order of inheritance being next after any relative in the same degree of the whole blood, and his issue, where the common ancestor is a male, and next after the common ancestor, where such common ancestor is a female. (See Steph. Comm. I. 15th ed. *et seq.*, also last Maxim and No. 203.)

98. Fraus est celare fraudem. *He who conceals a fraud perpetrates one himself.*

This illustrates the doctrine of constructive frauds. Where a man designedly produces a false impression on another, and the latter consequently commits some act, or enters into some contract, injurious to himself and his own interests, the former is guilty of fraud. (See Max. No. 260.)

99. Frustrâ fit per plura, quod fieri potest perpauciora. *That is unnecessarily done by many (words), which is capable of being done by fewer.*

That the force of this maxim has been appreciated by our legislature is shown and evidenced by most of the recent Acts of Parliament, and especially so by the Conveyancing and Law of Property Act, 1881, which has considerably curtailed the length of many legal documents. Accuracy and precision are ever to be commended in preference to verbosity. Short titles are now given to all important statutes.

100. Furiosus solo furore punitur. *Let a madman be punished by his madness alone.*

Thus, in general, idiots and lunatics are not liable on contracts, and bear a certain analogy to infants. (Chitty on Contracts, 16th ed.)

101. Generalis regula generaliter est intelligenda. *A general rule must be generally understood.*

102. Haereditas nunquam ascendit. *Inheritance never ascends.*

This rule was exploded by 3 & 4 Will. IV. c. 106, s. 6, by which, on failure of issue of the purchaser, the inheritance goes to the nearest lineal ancestor. Bracton and Lord Coke compared the descent of an inheritance to that of a falling body, which never went upwards in its course. "Descendit jus quasi ponderosum quid, cadens deorsum rectâ lineâ: et nunquam reascendit eâ viâ quâ descendit." (See Max. No. 58.)

103. Haeres legitimus est quam nuptiae demonstrant. *He is the legitimate heir whom marriage declares.*

*** 104. He who comes into equity must come with clean hands.**

An infant, although not generally liable on his contracts, cannot make use of his own fraudulent acts as a means whereby to benefit himself.

*** 105. He who seeks equity must do equity.**

It is in pursuance of this maxim that the right of the wife's equity to a settlement is enforced. (Snell's Eq. 16th ed.)

106. Hoc quidem perquam durum est, sed ita lex scripta est.
This indeed is hard, but it is the written law.

Although, in some cases, equity mitigated the rigours of the law, yet in others it was quite incapable of so doing; as, for example, many of the old laws of inheritance were certainly hard and unjust, yet equity gave no relief, the legislature having to intervene with the Act 3 & 4 Will. IV. c. 106.

107. Ibi esse poenam ubi et noxa est. *The punishment should be in the same place as the guilt.*

This is so according to the dictates of common sense and fairness.

*** 108. Id certum est quod certum reddi potest.** *That is certain which can be reduced to a certainty.*

This maxim is alike a rule of logic as of law. Customs must not be optional, but compulsory, reasonable, definite, &c.

109. Idem est non esse et non apparere. *Not to be and not to legally prove are the same thing.*

According to the laws of evidence, where he, on whom the onus of proving the affirmative lies, fails in such proof, the contrary is presumed, though there be no evidence in support of such presumption.

*** 110. Ignorantia facti excusat, ignorantia juris (quod quisque tenetur scire) neminem excusat.** *Ignorance of fact excuses, ignorance of the law (which every one is presumed to know) excuses no one.*

Applicable only to the general laws of the country *"quod quisque tenetur scire."* No action can be maintained to recover money paid under process of law. (See *Marriot* v. *Hampton,* 2 Sm. L. C. 421, and Snell's Eq. 16th ed. and Max. No. 176.)

111. In consimili casu, consimile debet esse remedium. *In similar cases, the remedy should be similar.*

(See Max. No. 265.)

*** 112. In contractu tacite insunt quæ sunt moris et consuetudinis.** *Those things which are customary and of general usage are tacitly implied in a contract.*

As a general rule, the law of the country in which a contract is entered into presumably governs its interpretation in the absence of a contrary and express intention of the parties. (*Jacob v. Crédit Lyonnaise,* 12 Q. B. D.)

113. In criminalibus probationes debent esse luce clariones.
In all criminal charges the proofs should be as clear as day.

An accused person is always entitled to receive the benefit of the doubt if any such exists on the evidence.

114. In judicio non creditur nisi juratis. *In a trial only sworn witnesses are believed.*

This has been modified of late years, especially by 17 & 18 Vict. c. 125, which, *inter alia*, provides that any person called as a witness, who shall refuse or be unwilling to be sworn from conscientious motives, may make affirmation instead. (As to the form of such affirmation, see 31 & 32 Vict. c. 72.)

*** 115. In jure, non remota, sed proxima spectantur.** *The law has regard to things near at hand, and not to those remote.*

Especially applicable in questions of damages, with reference to which one of the most important rules is, that they must not be too remote, but must be the natural and probable result of the defendant's wrongful act. Mayne on Damages says: "Damage is said to be too remote when, although arising out of the cause of action, it does not so immediately and necessarily flow from it, as that the offending party can be made responsible for it." (See also hereon *Hadley* v. *Baxendale*, 9 Ex. 343, and *Kelly* v. *Partington*, 5 B. & A. 645.)

116. In maleficiis voluntas spectatur non exitus. *In criminal acts the intention is to be sought or examined rather than the result.*

A bad or criminal intention must be shown in all such cases. (See Maxs. Nos. 9 and 285.)

*** 117. In pari delicto potior est conditio defendentis.** *In case of equal fault the position of the defendant is the better.*

Where an immoral contract has been executed, and both parties are equally in fault, the maxim applies, and the contract will not be set aside. In divorce actions, a wife guilty herself of adultery is not entitled to a decree *nisi* for which she may petition as against an offending husband. (See Chitty on Contracts, 16th ed. and next Max.)

118. In pari delicto potior est conditio possidentis. *In case of equal guilt, the condition of the possessor is the better.*

Where a marine policy is void, *ab initio*, from a cause not amounting to any fraud or breach of law on the part of the assured, the insurer is bound to return the premium paid; yet, when such policy is void by reason of fraud on the assured's part, the latter cannot then reclaim the premium, and the rule applies. (See Steph. Comm. II., and last Max.)

119. In presumptione juris semper æquitas existit. *Equity is always to be found in a presumption of law.*

Where the object of such presumption is satisfied, and there is no equity in continuing it, it should cease. (See *Colborne* v. *Patmore*, 4 Tyrwh. 677; C. M. & R. 73.)

120. In re communi potior est conditio prohibentis. *In a partnership the condition of one who forbids is the more favourable.*

When partners are equally divided, those who forbid any change or other alteration have the better right.

121. In societatis contractibus fides exuberet. *The strictest good faith must be exercised in partnership transactions.*

The highest standard of honour is requisite from every member of a partnership towards every other member of the firm.

122. In testamentus plenius testatoris intentionem scrutamur. *In wills we seek more especially for the testator's intention.*

This intention must be agreeable to law, and the intent must be collected from the actual words of the will. (See Maxs. Nos. 123, 273, and 275.)

123. In testamentis plenius voluntates testantium interpretantur. *In wills the wishes of testators are more liberally expounded.*

Thus Broom says: "A will should receive a more liberal construction than its strict meaning, if alone considered, would permit." (See Maxs. Nos. 122, 273, and 275.)

124. In traditionibus chartarum non quod dictum sed quod factum est inspicitur. *In the delivery of deeds, not what was said at the time, but what was done, must be looked at.*

A document under seal may be delivered to a third person only, to be delivered by him to the grantee, when the latter has performed certain specified conditions. Such documents are known as escrows, and do not acquire the force of a deed until the conditions precedent have been fulfilled and delivery thereupon made to the grantee. (See Steph. Comm. I. Cap. XVII., and Max. No. 264.)

125. Incertam et caducam haereditatem relevant. *They take up again a doubtful and lapsed inheritance.*

Upon the succession to a feud, on the death of the last tenant, the heir formerly succeeded thereto not as of right, but only by the favour of the lord of the manor, to whom a fine, called a relief, was paid—this relief continued payable even after feuds became hereditary, although the reason for its being claimed had ceased. (See Steph. Comm. Vol. I. Cap. II.)

126. Injuria non excusat injuriam. *One wrong does not justify another.* Or to use a colloquial expression, *Two wrongs will not make a right.*

127. Interest reipublicae, ut sit finis litium. *It is to the advantage of the State that there should be a limit to lawsuits.*

The Statutes of Limitations have been passed with a view to limit the time within which actions may be brought. But for these Statutes, a plaintiff might delay bringing his action until the defendant had lost, by casualty or otherwise, the evidence on which his case rested. (See Steph. Comm. III. Cap. XIII., and Max. No. 282.)

128. Invito beneficium non datur. *A benefit is not conferred upon an unwilling recipient.*

No one can be compelled to accept a gift against his wish. A legatee may refuse a gift, an executor may renounce probate, and a trustee may disclaim his office.

129. Judices non tenetur exprimere causam sententiae suae. *Judges are not compelled to give reason for their opinions; i.e., judgments or sentences.*

It is the general opinion that judges not only ought not to be compelled to explain, but also that they should not do so voluntarily. Recent years have witnessed a few instances in which an explanation has been vouchsafed; but it has been almost universally disapproved of by members of the legal profession.

130. Judicis est judicare secundum allegata et probata. *It is the duty of a judge to decide according to facts alleged and proved.*

In every action a litigant should be prepared to adduce proof of all facts upon which his case depends.

131. Judicis est jus dicere non dare. *It is for the judge to administer, not to make the law.*

Unwilling magistrates frequently shield themselves behind this, at times, very convenient rule.

132. Jura publica anteferenda privatis. *Public rights are to be preferred to private ones.*

133. Juris praecepta sunt haec: honeste vivere, alterum non laedere, suum cuique tribuere. *The maxims (or requirements) of the law are: To live honourably. To injure no one. To render to every one his due.*

*** 134. Jus accrescendi inter mercatores locum non habet, pro beneficio commercii.** *The right of survivorship has no existence among merchants, for the encouragement of trade.*

*** 135. Jus accrescendi praefertur oneribus ac ultimae voluntati.** *The right of survivorship is preferred to encumbrances and to the last will.*

This has reference to, and forms one of, the principal rules affecting joint tenancies. Dower and courtesy do not apply to joint estates.

136. Jus respicit aequitatem. *Law has regard to equity.*

(See Jud. Act, 1873, sec. 25, ss. 11, and Max. No. 141.)

137. Leges posteriores priores abrogant. *Subsequent laws repeal former ones.*

Statutes may repeal prior ones, either by express provision or by implication. Every statute impliedly repeals an earlier one, so far as the latter is contrary thereto. Unless otherwise expressed, a statute must be construed as prospective in its operation. (See Steph. Comm. I. and Max. No. 233.)

138. Leges solâ memoriâ et usu retinebant. *Laws were only preserved by memory and custom.*

Among the primitive Saxons, owing to the small skill in writing that generally obtained, all laws were traditional, being handed down from one generation to another solely by word of mouth. Our "unwritten" or Common Law of the present day, however, is not merely oral, but is to be sought in the records of the various Courts and in the reports of judicial decisions. (See Steph. Comm. I. sec. III.)

139. Lex non cogit ad impossibilia. *The law does not force to impossibilities.*

This rule does not apply where a thing is impossible on account only of the defendant's personal inability to perform a contract. (See Chitty on Contracts, 16th ed. and Max. 170.)

140. Lex prospicit non respicit. *The law looks forward, not backward.*

It is but seldom that statutes are made retrospective.

141. Lex respicit aequitatem. *The law has regard to equity.*

The provisions of the Judicature Acts are a good illustration. (See Max. No. 136.)

142. Linea recta semper praefertur transversali. *The right line is always preferred to the collateral.*

By 3 & 4 Will. IV. c. 106, "The lineal descendants *in infinitum* of any persons deceased shall represent their ancestor; that is, shall stand in the same place as the person himself would have done had he been living." The eldest male alone inherits where two or more are in equal degree of consanguinity to the purchaser; females inherit altogether. (See Williams on Real Property, 20th ed. Cap. IX.)

143. Littera scripta manet, vox emissa volat. *What is written endures, things spoken speed away.*

The distinction of damages in actions for libel and slander form a good illustration of what is meant by this maxim. (See Max. No. 286.)

144. Locus regit actum. *The place governs the act.*

The law of the place where a legal transaction was entered into—*Lex loci contractus*—usually governs its validity.

*** 145. Magis de bono quam de malo lex intendit.** *The law is in favour rather of a good than of a bad construction (or intention).*

If in a contract the words used are capable of two constructions, the one in conformity with, and the other against the law, the former is adopted. Every accused person is presumed in the law to be innocent until he be proved guilty. (See Chitty on Contracts, 16th ed., and Max. No. 169.)

146. Mala grammatica non vitiat chartam. *Bad grammar does not vitiate a deed or document.*

(See Chitty on Contracts, 16th ed. and Max. No. 89.)

147. Malus usus est abolendus. *An evil custom ought to be abolished.*

148. Melior est justicia vere praeveniens quam severe puniens. *Justice is better when it prevents rather than punishes with severity.*

149. Melius est petere fontes quam sectari rivulos. *It is better to go to the fountain head than to follow rivulets.*

All students will find this advice the best and safest to follow. (See Preface to this edition.)

150. Minatur innocentibus qui parcit nocentibus. *He who spares the guilty threatens the innocent.*

151. Minimè mutanda sunt quae certam habet interpretationem. *Such things as have a clear interpretation ought to be changed but little.*

This maxim is well illustrated by many of the old-fashioned technical terms used in conveyancing, and which by long usage have obtained a well-defined meaning, and one that cannot be well met by the use of any other word or expression, as the case may be.

*** 152. Mobilia sequuntur personam.** *Movables follow the person.*

On an intestacy, personal chattels are distributed according to the law of the country where deceased was domiciled at the time of death, and not according to the law of the place where they happen to be located.

*** 153. Modus et conventio vincunt legem.** *Custom and agreement override the law.*

This is one of the leading principles relative to the law of contracts. The exceptions to the rule here laid down are in cases against public policy, morality, &c. (See the case of *Richardson* v. *Langridge*, Tudor's L. C. Convey. 4th ed.; Chitty on Contracts, 16th ed. and Maxs. Nos. 37 and 197.)

154. Mors dicitur ultimum supplicium. *Death is said to be the extreme penalty.*

Death is the utmost limit of all things. Capital punishment is now only inflicted in cases of high treason and murder.

155. Multi multa, nemo omnia novit. *Many have known many things; no one has known everything.*

So long, at least, as the law is ever changing, this must remain true.

156. Mutatis mutandis. *Making such changes or alterations as the sense requires.*

157. Nam silent leges inter arma. *Laws are silent in time of war.*

It is to be noticed that during those periods of our history in which wars, civil or foreign, were most prevalent, very little was accomplished in the way of legislature. Domestic legislation is always a sure index of a peaceful administration.

158. Necessitas non habet legem. *Necessity has no law.*

(See next Max.)

159. Necessitas vincit legem. *Necessity defeats the law.*

(See last Max. and No. 230.)

160. Nemo contra factum suum venire potest. *No one can go against his own deed.*

This maxim illustrates the doctrine of estoppel, of which there are three kinds. (1) By matter of record; (2) by deed; (3) by matter in pais. No person can, after execution, dispute his own solemn deed, which is conclusive against him and those claiming under him, even as to facts recited therein. (See Chitty on Contracts, 16th ed.)

161. Nemo dat quod non habet. *No one can give what he has not.*

No one can, other than by sale in market overt, confer upon another a better title than he himself has. A great exception to this principle occurs in the case of "negotiable securities," which by custom are transferable like cash by delivery. (See *Miller* v. *Race*, 1 Sm. L. C.) A thief can confer no title to stolen goods. (See Maxs. Nos. 166 and 232.)

162. Nemo de domo suâ extrahi potest. *No man can be dragged out of his own house.*

(See Max. No. 62.)

163. Nemo debet bis punari, pro uno delicto. *No one should be twice punished for the same offence.*

(See next Max.)

* **164. Nemo debet bis vexari pro unâ et eâdem causâ.** *No one ought to be tried twice (twice put to trouble) for one and the same cause.*

It is a well-established principle of Criminal Law, that where a man is indicted for an offence and acquitted, he cannot afterwards be again indicted for the same offence, if he might have been convicted at the onset by proof of the facts contained in the second indictment. (See last Max.)

* **165. Nemo est haeres viventis.** *No man is heir of a living person.*

There may be either an heir apparent, as the eldest son, or an heir presumptive, as an only daughter. The question of actual heirship arises only on the death of the owner. No inheritance can vest, and no one can be a complete heir until the ancestor is dead. (See Max. No. 59.)

* **166. Nemo plus juris in alium transferre potest quam ipse habet.** *No one can confer a better right to another than he has himself.*

(But see *Miller* v. *Race*, 1 Sm. L. C. 11th ed.and Max. No. 161.)

167. Nemo potest esse agens et patiens. *No one can be alike an active and a passive party.*

* **168. Nemo potest mutare consilium suum in alterius injuriam.** *No one can change his purpose (or advice) to the injury of another.*

It will be noticed that Acts of Legislation are generally prospective and not retrospective in their application. The doctrine of estoppel also illustrates the meaning intended to be conveyed.

169. Nemo praesumitur malus. *No one is presumed to be bad.*

(See Max. No. 145.)

> *** 170. Nemo tenetur ad impossibile.** *No one is bound to an impossibility.*

If a man contracts to do anything which is physically impossible, such contract is not binding on him; but where the contract is to do a thing which, though possible at the time, subsequently becomes impossible, it is otherwise; also if the impossibility is one personal only to the contractor. (See Max. No. 139.)

> **171. Nemo tenetur seipsum prodere.** *No one is bound to betray himself; i.e., cannot be compelled to criminate himself.*

A well recognised rule of evidence in all cases. (See Max. No. 3.)

> **172. Nihil tam conveniens est naturali aequitati, quam unumquodque dissolvi eo ligamine quo legatum est.** *Nothing is so consonant to natural equity, as that a thing may be dissolved by the same means which made it binding.*

> **173. Non accipi debent verba in demonstrationem falsam quae competunt in limitationem veram.** *Words which admit of a true meaning ought not to be received in a false sense, or one inconsistent with the facts.*

Thus, where there is a subject-matter which answers in every particular to a description contained in a will or deed, no part of the description can be rejected so as to make it include more.

> **174. Non est regula quin fallat.** *There is no rule but it may fail; exception proves the rule.*

(See Max. No. 83)

> **175. Non quod dictum est, sed quod factum est, inspicitur.** *Regard is to be had, not to what is said, but to what is done.*

Where a lessor gives a receipt for money tendered to him as rent, this is in point of law a receipt for rent, and a waiver of any forfeiture which may have been previously incurred; although the lessor, before the tender, and on taking the rent, expressed his intention to accept the money only as compensation for the use of the land. (*Croft* v. *Lumley*, 5 E. & B. 648.)

> **176. Non videntur qui errant consentire.** *Those who make a mistake are not considered to consent.*

Mistake is of two kinds, either of fact or of law, the former, as a rule, will be relieved against "*Ignorantia facti excusat*," provided there had been no acquiescence; but with regard to the latter the Court will only grant relief in exceptional cases, "*Ignorantia legis neminem excusat*." (See *Lansdowne*

v. *Lansdowne*, 2 Jacob & Walker, 205.) Ignorance of foreign law is deemed ignorance of fact. (See generally hereon Snell's Eq. 16th ed. and Max. No. 110.)

177. Noscitur a sociis. *It may be known or explained from its associates; i.e., the meaning may often be gathered from the context ("si non cognoscitur ex se").*

This refers to the construction of words and clauses in contracts and written instructions. (See Chitty on Contracts, 16th ed. and Max. No. 78.)

178. Nudum pactum. *A naked agreement; i.e., a bare promise; a contract not supported by necessary consideration.*

179. Nullum scutaglum ponatur in regno nostro, nisi per communes consilium regni nostris. *No scutage can be imposed in our realm, save by the common council of the kingdom.*

All imperial taxes are fixed and settled by the House of Commons, in which House all "money Bills" originate.

*** 180. Nullum tempus aut locus occurrit Regi.** *No time or place affects the king.*

Lapse of time will not generally bar the right of the Crown.

181. Nullus clericus nisi causidicus. *A clerk (in holy orders) was ever a pleader.*

In early times the clergy monopolised all learning, and out of their ranks all judges were formally appointed, all the inferior legal offices being also filled by the lower clergy: hence their name of clerks. From the year 1373–1530 A.D. no lawyer filled the office of Lord Chancellor, the post being all along occupied by the clergy. *"Les juges sont sages personnes et autentiques, sicomme, les archevesques, evesques, les chanoines, &c."*

*** 182. Nullus commodum capere potest de injuria sua propriâ.** *No one can obtain an advantage by his own wrong.*

The examples of this maxim are numerous in every branch of the law. (See *Twyne's Case*, 1 Sm. L. C. 11th ed. and Maxs. Nos. 80 and 82.)

183. Nullus simile est idem, nisi quotuor pedibus currit. *No like is exactly identical unless it runs on all fours.*

184. Obiter dictum. *Said by the way; i.e., in passing.*

The *"obiter dicta"* of learned judges are frequently quoted, although the same do not directly relate to the actual facts upon which judgment is being delivered, consequently they are not so important.

185. Odiosa et inhonesta non sunt praesumunda in lege. *Odious and dishonest things are not to be presumed in law.*

186. Officium nemini debet esse damnosum. *A duty should be injurious to no one.*

No one should sustain any loss by reason of doing his duty. Thus, Justices of the Peace and County Court bailiffs should not personally suffer loss on account of their having, in the performance of their duty, to do things which are sometimes distasteful alike to themselves and others.

*** 187. Omne majus continet in se minus.** *The greater contains the less.*

A tender by a debtor to his creditor of an amount in excess of that owing is perfectly good for what is actually due. (See Chitty on Contracts, 16th ed.)

188. Omne quod solo inaedificatur solo cedit. *Everything built on the soil belongs to the soil.*

The grant of certain land will pass to the grantee all buildings and erections thereon, even though such erections be not specifically mentioned. (See Steph. Comm. I. and Maxs. Nos. 46 and 224.)

*** 189. Omne testamentum morte consummatum est, et voluntas testatoris est ambulatoria usque ad mortem.**
Every testament is perfected by death, and the will of a testator is "ambulatory" (revocable) even unto death.

A will is of no effect and does not operate until the death of the testator, until which time it may be revoked or altered by him at his pleasure. It speaks from the date of death, and not that of its execution.

A will may be defined as follows:—Voluntatis nostrae justa sententia de eo quod quis post mortem suam fieri velet. (See Max. No. 261.)

190. Omnia praesumuntur contra spoliatorem. *Every presumption is made against a wrongdoer.*

See the third point of decision in *Armory* v. *Delamirie*, 1 Sm. L. C. 11th ed. where it was decided that if a person withhold evidence in his possession, every presumption shall be adopted to his disadvantage, that is, such evidence shall be taken as adverse to his interest.

*** 191. Omnia praesumuntur rite et solenniter esse acta, donec probetur in contrarium.** *All things are presumed to have been rightly and properly performed, until the contrary is proved.*

Where there is a proper attestation clause to a will which appears on the face of it to be duly executed, the Court assumes that the Wills Act has been complied with, even although the witnesses may forget the circumstances. (See *Vinnicombe* v. *Butler*, 34 L. J. (P. & M.) 18.)

192. Omnis coactio a legato abesse debet. *Every suit against an ambassador should fail.*

It has now been decided that an ambassador is entitled to absolute exemption from suits in the Courts of the country to which he is sent. (See *The Magdalene Steam Navigation Co.* v. *Martin,* 2 El. & El. 94, 28 L. J. Q. B. 310.)

193. Omnis innovatio plus novitate perturbat quam utilitate prodest. *Every innovation occasions more harm by its novelty than benefit by its utility.*

The principle here laid down applies rather to the immediate, than to the ultimate and permanent effects. (See *Ashby* v. *White,* 1 Smith, L. C. 11th ed. and Chitty on Contracts, 16th ed.)

*** 194. Omnis ratihabitio retrotrahitur et mandato priori aequiparatur.** *Every ratification has a retrospective effect and is equivalent to a previous authority or contract.*

Where a person acts as agent for another, and professes (without authority) to contract for him, a subsequent assent by the principal is equivalent to a previous authority. (See Chitty on Contracts, 16th ed. also Maxs. Nos. 55 and 208.)

195. Omnium contributione sarciatur quod per omnibus datum est. *That which is given for all should be contributed by all.*

This maxim is the essence of the law as to general average, under which, where goods have been thrown overboard for the safety of a ship, that being the only alternative, contribution to the loss is made proportionately by the owners of the ship and all who have goods on board. (See Steph. Comm. II. Cap. V. Sec. X.)

*** 196. Once a mortgage always a mortgage.** *Where a document is once satisfactorily established as a mortgage, a mortgage it always will remain.*

This was not formerly so at Common Law, but now, since the Judicature Act, 1873, the rule of equity prevails. (See Snell's Eq. 16th ed. and Max. No. 74.)

197. Optimus legis interpres est consuetudo. *Custom is the best interpreter of law.*

(See also Maxs. Nos. 37 and 153.)

198. Pacta privata juri publico derogare non possunt. *Private contracts cannot repeal the public right—i.e., cannot adversely affect a public right.*

*** 199. Partus sequitur ventrem.** *The offspring follows the womb.*

This maxim illustrates the doctrine of property arising from accession, and is grounded on the right of occupancy. It has been held in the case of all tame and domestic animals, that the offspring belong to the owner of the mother, although in the case of human beings it is otherwise, except as to bastards. (See Steph. Comm. II.)

200. Patria potestas in pietate debet, non in atrocitate, consistere. *A father's power ought to be based on affection and not on cruelty.*

Parents' power over their children is derived from their duty towards them, being given them, partly to enable them the more effectually to perform their duty, and partly as a recompense for their trouble in its discharge. (See Steph. Comm. II. Cap. III., also the recent Acts for the Prevention of Cruelty to Children.)

201. Pendente lite nihil innovetur. *Whilst a lawsuit is pending nothing must be altered.*

This principle or effect is limited to the rights of parties in that particular suit.

202. Pluris est occulatus testis usus quam auriti decem. *One eye-witness is worth more than ten hearsay.*

Hearsay or second-hand evidence is generally inadmissible except in certain cases, such as questions of custom or pedigree.

203. Possessio fratris (de feodo simplici) facit sororem esse haeredem. *Possession by the brother of an estate in fee simple constitutes the sister heiress.*

Applicable to the old law of inheritance, under which the half-blood were totally excluded from the succession, land descending to a sister of the whole blood of the person last seised, rather than to a brother of the half-blood. Now, however, by 3 & 4 Will. IV. c. 106, the half-blood are admitted. (See Steph. Comm. I. also Maxs. Nos. 96 and 97.)

204. Potior est conditio possidentis. *The condition of one in possession is the more preferable.*

The old English adage, "Possession is nine-tenths of the law," now very qualified in its truth and application, probably had its origin in this maxim. (See Max. No. 118.)

205. Praestat cautela quam medela. *Caution is better than cure.*

206. Principia probant non probantur. *It is not necessary to prove first principles—i.e.,* maxims (see Preface).

207. Quaelibet concessio fortissime contra donatorem interpretanda est. *Every grant is to be interpreted most strongly against the donor.*

(See Max. No. 272.)

*** 208. Quando aliquid mandatur, mandatur et omne per quod pervenitur ad illud.** *When anything is ordered to be done, everything by which it is to be accomplished is also impliedly authorised.*

One of the rules affecting the law of principal and agent, is that the latter's authority includes all medium powers "per quod pervenitur ad illud."

209. Quando jus domini regis et subditi concurrunt jus regis praeferri debet. *When the right of the king and that of a subject arise simultaneously the former takes precedence.*

*** 210. Quando lex aliquid alicui concedit, concedere videtur et id sine quo res ipsa esse non potest.** *When the law gives a man anything it gives him that also without which the thing itself cannot exist.*

Under the following circumstances a *way of necessity* is implied—*e.g.*, if A. grant to B. a piece of land surrounded on all sides by other land of A.'s B. will (in case there be no right of way to his land) have a right of way over A.'s surrounding land for such time as the necessity exists. The application of this maxim is very limited, and it refers more especially to contracts under seal. (See Chitty on Contracts, 16th ed. and Max. No. 42.)

*** 211. Quando res non valet ut ago, valeat quantum valere potest.** *When anything does not operate in the way one intends, let it operate as far as it can.*

In the case of *Roe* v. *Tranmarr*, 2 Sm. L. C. a deed purporting to be a release which could not operate as such because it attempted to convey a freehold "in futuro," was held valid under the circumstances as a covenant to stand seised (see Max. No. 26). A lease in writing but not under seal, is not absolutely void, but held good in equity as an agreement for a lease. (See Maxs. Nos. 271, 273, and 275.)

212. Qui ex damnato coitu nascuntur inter liberos non computantur. *Those born from an unlawful intercourse are not to be deemed among the lawful children.*

Bastards are incapable under our law of being heirs, and are held to be "nullius filii." By the civil law they could inherit being legitimated by the lawful marriage of their fathers and mothers.

* **213. Qui facit per alium facit per se.** *He who acts through*
another acts through himself.

A contract made by an agent is looked upon in law as the contract of
the principal, so agents need not be "*sui juris*," and infants, married women,
and others are competent to act as such. The agent must, however, act within
the scope of his authority. In *Scott* v. *Shepherd*, 2 Black. 892, an action was
held to lie against the person who originally threw a squib which, after being
knocked about by other persons in self-defence, ultimately hit and put out the
plaintiff's eye. (See Chitty on Contracts, 16th ed. and Max. No. 240.)

214. Qui haeret in litera haeret in cortice. *He who considers*
only the mere wording of a document goes but skin deep into its
meaning.

(See Maxs. Nos. 26, 78, 177, and 273.)

215. Qui minimum probat nihil probat. *He proves nothing who*
proves too much.

216. Qui non improbat, approbat. *He who does not blame,*
approves.

(See next Max.)

* **217. Qui non prohibet id quod prohibere potest, assentire**
videtur. *He who does not forbid what he is able to prevent, appears*
to assent.

So one who enables another to commit a fraud is answerable. A person
who has a title to property offered for sale at an auction, and, knowing his
title, stands by and encourages the sale or does not forbid it, will be bound
by the sale, for "*Qui non obstat quod obstare potest, facere videtur.*" *Teasdale* v.
Teasdale, Sel. Ch. Cas. 59. (See Snell's Eq. 16th ed. cap. 3, and also Maxs. Nos.
35, 98, 216, and 222.)

218. Qui parcit nocentibus, innocentes punit. *He who spares*
the guilty, punishes the innocent.

219. Qui peccat ebrius, luat sobrius. *Let him who sins when*
drunk, be punished when sober.

An intoxicated person can derive no privilege from a madness thus
voluntarily contracted. On an indictment for murder, however, intoxication
may be taken into consideration, to show that the act was not premeditated,
and if there has been some contrivance or inducement to allure the party
into drink, or any unfair advantage taken of his intoxication, the Court will
sometimes relieve. (But see Chitty on Contracts, 16th ed.)

*** 220. Qui prior est tempore potior est jure.** *He who is first in point of time is preferred in law.*

(See *Brace* v. *Duchess of Marlborough*, 2 P. Wms. 49 1, and *Marsh* v. *Lee*, 2 Wh. and Tud. L. C. Eq. 8th ed.) Subject to the provisions of the Conveyancing and Law of Property Act, 1881, a mortgagee may recover in ejectment without giving notice to quit against a tenant who claims under a lease from the mortgagor, granted after the mortgage without the privity of the mortgagee. The rule stated in this maxim applies as between finders of "treasure trove," derelicts, and such like. (See also *Keech* v. *Hall*, 1 Sm. L. C. 11th ed.) Where several persons have interests in the same property, and equal equities in every point except time, as in the case of a third mortgagee who had no notice of a second mortgage when making his advance, here both mortgagees have equal equities, but the second mortgagee, being first in point of time, has the prior right. In this instance, however, the third mortgagee could avail himself of the advantages of tacking. (See Max. No. 288, and Snell, 16th ed.)

*** 221. Qui sentit commodum sentire debet et onus.** *He who receives the advantage ought also to suffer the burden.*

Equity always acted on this principle when enforcing contribution between co-sureties. (*Dering* v. *Earl of Winchilsea*, 2 Wh. and Tud. L. C. Eq. 8th ed. 539, and *Waugh* v. *Carver*, 2 Hen. *Blackstone*, 235; *Cox* v. *Hickman*, 1 Sm. L. C. 414.)

222. Qui tacet sentire videtur. *He who is silent appears to consent.*

(See Maxs. Nos. 35, 216, 217.)

223. Qui vult decipi, decipiatur. *Let him be deceived who wishes to be deceived.*

A person who has been guilty of such gross negligence as to court deception will obtain no relief from the Court. (See Maxs. Nos. 47 and 61.)

*** 224. Quicquid plantatur solo solo cedit.** *Whatever is planted in (or affixed to the soil) belongs to the soil.*

This principle is stringently adhered to as between the heir-at-law and the executor of a deceased person, and as between mortgagors and mortgagees; but it has been very considerably relaxed in its application to fixtures as between landlord and tenant. (See Chitty on Contracts, 16th ed. and Maxs. Nos. 46 and 188.)

*** 225. Quicquid solvitur, solvitur secundum modum solventis, quicquid recipitur, recipitur secundum modum recipientis.** *Whatever money is paid, is paid according to the* *direction of the payer, whatever money received, is received according to that of the recipient.*

A debtor has, at the time of payment, the first right to direct the same to be appropriated in liquidation of whatever debt due to his creditor he chooses. If the debtor omit to do this, the creditor has the next right of appropriation to what debt he chooses. If neither party makes appropriation, the law makes it—generally to the earlier debt. (See Rule in Clayton's Case and Snell's Eq. 16th ed.)

226. Quisque suâ acte perito est credendum. *Every one experienced in his own calling is to be believed.*

(See Max. No. 43.)

*** 227. Quod ab initio non valet, in tractu temporis non convalescit.** *That which was void from its commencement, does not improve by lapse of time.*

Where any contract amounts to a constructive fraud, on account of its being opposed to some positive law, or public policy, it is void and incapable of ratification—it is different, however, when the contract is voidable only.

228. Quod fieri non debuit factum valet. *That which ought not to be done, is yet valid (sometimes) when done.*

Money paid in pursuance of an illegal contract which has been performed cannot, as a rule, be recovered back. (See also Max. No. 93.)

229. Quod naturalis ratio inter homines constituit vocatur jus gentium. *That which by natural reason prevails among men is called the law of nations.*

International law is not grounded upon the caprice of any particular nation, but depends entirely upon mutual compacts and treaties between the various States. The construction also of such compacts is governed by the law of nations, being the only one to which all communities are equally amenable. Civil Law, as distinguished from International Law, is thus defined: "*Jus civili, est quod quisque sibi populus constituit.*"

230. Quod necessitas cogit, excusat. *That which necessity compels, she excuses.*

A person is not held criminally responsible for actions which he is forced to commit under threats of death or grievous bodily harm, continuing during the whole time of the commission of such acts. This non-liability, however, does not extend to cases where the death of an innocent person results. (See *Reg.* v. *M'Growther*, 18 St. Tr. 394, and Maxs. Nos. 158 and 159.)

231. Quod nullius est, est domini regis. *What is the property of no one, belongs to the king.*

Land will go to the Crown on the decease of the last owner or person actually seised intestate, and without heirs. So also do waifs (*bona vacantia*), and unclaimed wreckage. (See Wills Act.)

> **232. Quod per me non possum, nec per alium.** *That which one cannot himself do, he cannot do by another.*

No one can delegate a power which he himself does not possess. (See Max. No. 161.)

> **233. Quod populus postremum jussit, id jus ratum esto.** *That which a people has last ordained shall be the established law.*

(See Steph. Comm. I. and Max. No. 137.)

> *** 234. Quod turpi ex causâ promissum est, non valet.** *An immoral (illegal or base) consideration will not support a promise (i.e., a contract).*

So also one founded on an impossible or purely moral consideration.

(See Chitty on Contracts, 16th ed. and Maxs. Nos. 80 and 82.)

> *** 235. Quoties in verbis nulla est ambiguitas, ibi nulla expositio contra verba fienda est.** *When there is no ambiguity in the language of an instrument, no interpretation is to be made contrary to the words.*

It is a rule that parol evidence contrary to the express written language itself is excluded, and the instrument itself is the only criterion of the intention of the parties. Parol evidence may be admissible to explain, but not to contradict or override, the express written contents of an instrument.

(See Chitty on Contracts, 16th ed.)

> **236. Quoties idem sermo duas sententias exprimit ea potissimum accipiatur, quae rei gerendae aptior est.** *When the same expression carries two meanings, that shall be preferred which is the more fitted to elucidate the subject-matter.*

This is one of the numerous rules for the construction of legal documents. (See Max. No. 26.)

> **237. Res ipse loquitur.** *The thing speaks for itself (without proof).*

Frequently quoted in actions for damages for negligence. (See Max. No. 69, and Chitty on Contracts, 16th ed.)

> **238. Res inter alios acta alteri nocere non debet.** *A thing done between two persons ought not to injure another.*

(See *Duchess of Kingston's Case*, 2 Sm. L. C. 731.)

> **239. Res judicata pro veritate accipiatur.** *A point judicially decided is taken to be correct.*

This is conclusive so far as Courts of inferior jurisdiction are concerned, until the judgment is reversed.

*** 240. Respondeat superior.** *Let the principal answer.*

One authorising an unlawful act to be done by his servant, is himself answerable. The maxim does not apply as against the Crown. See also Max. No. 213. Also "Qui per alium facit per seipsum facere videtur." Also the case of *Thompson* v. *Davenport*, 2 Sm. L. C. Where at the time of sale the vendor is aware that there is a principal, but does not know who he is and debits the agent, he may nevertheless resort to the principal when known.

241. Rex debet esse sub lege, quia lex facit regem. *The king ought to be subservient to the law, for the law makes the king.*

This is so in our realm at the present time, although many of our earlier Sovereigns appeared to think otherwise, and acted accordingly.

242. Rex in suo regno non habet parum. *In his own kingdom the king has no equal.*

243. Rex nunquam moritur. *The king never dies.*

The person only is changed, but the Sovereign always exists—*i.e.*, the Crown never falls vacant.

244. Rex peccare non potest. *The king can do no wrong.*

245. Salus populi est suprema lex. *The public safety (welfare) is the supreme law.*

The prosperity of its people, and the proper maintenance of order and security, as also the diffusion of domestic and social happiness, should be the first and main object of every government.

246. Scientia utrinque par pares contrahentes facit. *Equal knowledge on both sides makes the position of the contracting parties the same.*

In an insurance policy there are many things relating to the subject-matter thereof as to which the insured can be innocently silent—for instance, he need not mention any facts within the insurer's own knowledge; for an insurer cannot insist that a policy is void because the insurer did not inform him that which he already knew.

247. Scire debes cum quo contrabis. *One should know with whom he contracts.*

This is self-evident, so that a person may know whom to sue and look to for damages in case of a breach of the contract.

248. Scribere est agere. *To write is the same thing as to act.*

A deed in writing is, at the present time, sufficient to effect the transfer of property, without any actual livery of seisin.

> *** 249. Seisina (non jus) facit stipitem.** *Seisin (not the law) makes the root of descent.*

This was formerly a most important maxim, but the doctrine is exploded by the Inheritance Act, 3 & 4 Will. IV. c. 106, which enacts that "Descent shall in all cases be traced from the last purchaser, whether he may or may not have actually obtained possession." The purchaser is defined by the Act as being the last person who had a right to the land who cannot be proved to have acquired the land by descent, or by certain means which render the land part of, or descendible in the same manner as other land acquired by descent (*e.g.*, escheat, partition, or enclosure). Under the old law no one could be such an ancestor as to have descent traced from him, unless he had been in actual possession of the land, or in receipt of the rents and profits prior to his death.

> **250. Semper in dubiis benigniora praeferenda.** *In doubtful matters the more liberal (constructions) are to be preferred.*

(See Max. No. 26.)

> **251. Semper in obscuris quod minimum est sequimur.** *In obscure (constructions) the law follows that which is least obscure.*

(*Williams* v. *Crosling*, 3 C. B. 962, and Max. No. 26.)

> **252. Semper praesumitur pro negante.** *Presumption is ever in favour of the negative.*

The "onus probandi" lies on the plaintiff (see Maxs. Nos. 24 and 69). It is also to be remembered that every one is presumed in law to be innocent until the contrary is proved.

> **253. Si plura sint debita, vel plus legatum fuerit, ad quae catalla defuncti non sufficiant, fiat ubique defalcatio, excepto regis privilegio.** *If the debts or legacies of a deceased are greater than the assets will satisfy, the same shall abate rateably, the privilege of the Crown excepted.*

If the assets of a deceased person are insufficient to pay the debts and the legacies bequeathed by his will, all the general legacies abate rateably. A specific legacy, as of a piece of plate, is not liable to abatement, until the fund applicable for general legacies is exhausted; but, on the other hand, it is liable to ademption—*i.e.*, it may have been otherwise disposed of by the testator in his lifetime. Debts in every case form a first charge on the estate. (See Steph. Comm. II.)

> *** 254. Sic utere tuo ut alienum non laedas.** *So enjoy your own rights as not to injure those of another.*

Where the natural course of a stream is over the surface of lands belonging to different proprietors, no proprietor above can diminish the quantity or injure the quality of the water which descends; nor can a proprietor below throw back the water without licences from the proprietors above. *Aedificare in tuo proprio solo non licet quod alteri noceat.*

255. Simplex commendatio non obligat. *Mere recommendation will not render a man liable.*

Where a purchaser is satisfied without express warranty, a mere representation of the quality by the seller will not entitle him to recover, unless he can show the same to have been fraudulently made. (See *Chandelor* v. *Lopus*, 1 Sm. L. C. and Max. No. 28.)

256. Socius mei socii, socius meus non est. *The partner of my partner is not necessarily my partner.*

257. Statuta pro publico commodo late interpretantur. *Statutes passed for the public good should be construed literally.*

258. Sublata causâ, tollitur effectus. *The cause being gone, the effect also ceases.*

This is a fact applicable alike to law as to physics.

259. Summum jus, summa injuria. *Where the law is most strictly administered, it sometimes causes the greatest wrong.*

It frequently happens that a plaintiff or defendant loses his case, although morally in the right, on account of some technicality which has not been observed.

*** 260. Suppressio veri suggestio est falsi.** *Withholding the truth suggests falsehood.*

(See also Max. No. 98.)

261. Testamentum omne morte consummatur. *Every will is perfected by death.*

A will speaks from the time of death only. (See Max. No. 189.)

262. Testes ponderantur, non numerantur. *Witnesses are weighed (considered at their proper worth), not numbered.*

The evidence of one credible witness counts for more than that of any number who cannot be relied upon.

263. Testis nemo in suâ causâ esse potest. *No one can be a witness on his own behalf.*

This rule applies to criminal charges, and its effect is continually being modified by legislation. The opinion of those best qualified to judge, differs whether or not all accused persons should not be competent witnesses.

264. Traditio loqui facit chartam. *The delivery of a deed makes it effectual.*

The delivery of a deed is equally important with the signing and sealing. Both the delivery and sealing are performed at the present day, by placing the finger on the seal and repeating the words, "I deliver this as my act and deed." A delivery may be either absolute or conditional. (See Steph. Comm. I. Cap. XVII., and Max. No. 124.)

265. Ubi eadem ratio, ibi eadem lex; et de similibus idem est judicium. *Where there is the same reason, there is the same law; and concerning things similar, the judgment is similar.*

(See Max. No. 111.)

*** 266. Ubi jus ibi remedium.** *There is no wrong without a remedy, or, Where there is a legal right there is a remedy.*

An action will lie for an injury although no actual damage be sustained, as in the case of *Ashby* v. *White* (temp. 2 Anne, 1704, 14 State Trials, 695), where it was decided that an action lay against a returning officer for refusing to admit the vote of a duly qualified elector, although the persons for whom he tendered his votes were elected. There may be a *"damnum absque injuriâ"* (loss without a wrongful act) for which no action will lie. Thus no action will lie against one's neighbour, who builds on his own land a mill, whereby the profits of one's own mill (built on adjoining property) are diminished, although in the case put considerable loss may result. This maxim formed the root of all equitable decisions, and was the basis upon which the Court of Chancery originally acted, when interfering with Courts of Law, or in supplying remedies for those wrongs which the latter failed to redress.

267. Ubi nullum matrimonium, ibi nulla dos. *Where there is no marriage, there is no dower.*

A woman, in order to be entitled to dower on the death of her husband, must have been his actual wife at the time of his decease: there must have been no dissolution of the marriage. The law as to dower is now governed by 3 & 4 Will. IV. c. 105. (See Steph. Comm. I.)

268. Unum est tacere, aliud celare. *To be silent or to conceal are two different things.*

A party to a contract is not bound to disclose latent defects, but he must not fraudulently conceal, or the contract will be voidable. The rule as to defects that are patent to all is otherwise.

269. Unumquodque dissolvitur eodem modo quo colligatum est. *Every obligation can only be dissolved in the same manner as it was created.*

Thus a deed can only be revoked by deed, and not by a simple written instrument. This, of course, subject to the ruling of Courts of competent jurisdiction.

270. Utile per inutile non vitiatur. *That which is useful is not vitiated by that which is useless.*

Where the meaning of any document is clear, its effect is not marred or upset by the insertion therein of superfluous and meaningless words.

271. Valeat quantum valere potest. *Let it stand as far as possible. Let it pass for what it is worth.*

(See Max. No. 211.)

*** 272. Verba chartarum fortius accipiuntur contra proferentem.** *Words of deeds or grants are to be taken most strongly against the grantor.*

Thus, a rent of 10s. granted by tenants in common is several, and the grantee will have 10s. from each: aliter if a rent of 10s. be reserved. This principle does not apply to a grant by the Crown at the suit of the grantee. Nor must such a rule of construction be followed till all others fail, for the law supposes that a person will not use language to his own detriment. (See Chitty on Contracts, 16th ed. and Maxs. Nos. 18 and 207.)

*** 273. Verba debent intelligi cum effectu, ut res magis valeat quam pereat.** *Words ought to be understood with effect, that a thing may rather be preserved than destroyed.*

(See *Roe* v. *Tranmarr*, 2 Sm. L. C. 506.) This rule is closely allied to *Benignae faciendae sunt interpretationes chartarum ut res magis valeat quam pereat.* (The construction of deeds shall be made liberally that the subject-matter may rather prevail than perish.) Construction must in all cases be reasonable, liberal, and favourable. (See Chitty on Contracts, 16th ed. and Maxs. Nos. 26, 78, 145, and 275.)

*** 274. Verba generalia restringuntur ad habilitatem rei vel aptitudinem personae.** *General words must be narrowed either to the nature of the subject-matter or to the capability of the person.*

Such words must be understood with reference to the estate which is in the grantor at the time of the grant. Thus a bill of sale which purported to assign to R. "all the household goods and furniture of every kind and description in a certain house, and more particularly mentioned and set forth in an inventory or schedule of even date therewith," was held to apply only to the goods specified in the inventory which did not comprise all the goods in the house. In construing a statute general words must not be extended unduly. (See Chitty on Contracts, 16th ed. and Max. No. 88.)

* **275. Verba intentioni debent inservire.** *Words ought to be made subservient to the intention—i.e., should be construed so as to give effect to the intention—"ut res magis valeat quam pereat."*

(*Roe* v. *Tranmarr*, 2 Sm. L. C. 506.) The rule laid down in this maxim is one of the first and most important in the construction of contracts, so that they may be enforced according to the sense in which the parties mutually intended. Words and expressions are to be understood in their plain, ordinary, and popular sense, unless they may by custom of trade or the like have acquired a peculiar or technical sense and meaning. The "golden rule" as regards Acts of Parliament is that the words must be construed in their plain and grammatical sense and as mentioned in the preceding paragraph. (See Chitty on Contracts, 16th ed. and Maxs. Nos. 26, 39, 122, and 273.)

276. Verba relata in esse videntur. *Words referred to are deemed to be incorporated.*

Where a father infeoff his son, to have and to hold to him and his heirs, and the son then infeoff his father, purporting to do so only *as fully as his father infeoffed him*, by this, the father has a fee simple. On this same principle, existing but unattested papers, or documents, may be incorporated in a will, if referred to in such a way as to render their identity indisputable.

277. Veritas nominis tollit errorem demonstrationis.
Correctness in the name removes an error of demonstration.

In the construction of wills, this rule has frequently been acted on, but it must be first shown that there is an error of demonstration; until when the above maxim has, of course, no application. (See *Drake* v. *Drake*, 8 House of Lords Cases, 172; also 2 Smith, L. C.)

278. Vetustas pro lege semper habetur. *An old custom is ever regarded as law.*

279. Via trita est tutissima. *The beaten track is the safest.*

This is a good and safe rule to follow, but has its "proving exceptions" in the many originators, scientists, &c., of whom England is so justly proud.

280. Vicarius non habet vicarium. *A locum tenens (i.e., substitute) cannot appoint another in his stead.*

(See Max. No. 55.)

*** 281. Victus victori in expensis condemnandus est.** *The loser must defray the costs of a successful litigant.*

By the Judicature Acts, in the case of a trial by jury, costs follow the event, unless the judge shall, for good cause, order otherwise, but in all other cases, they are in the discretion of the Court. (See Steph. Comm. III.)

*** 282. Vigilantibus et non dormientibus succurrunt jura** (or **æquitas subvenit**). *Laws come to the help of the vigilant, not of the sleepy* (also written *"equity assists the vigilant,"* &c.).

Before relieving a party from a contract on the ground of fraud, it must be shown to the Court that he exercised a due degree of caution before entering into such contract. The misrepresentation must be material, and the party claiming relief have been misled by it. It is not essential that the person making the false statement should know it to be such. The Statutes of Limitations are founded on the principle that a dilatory claimant deserves no assistance. (See Chitty on Contracts, 16th ed. and Max. No. 127.)

*** 283. Volenti non fit injuria.** *No injury can be done to a willing person.*

If a person voluntarily consents to an injury, he must bear the loss. A woman cannot herself support an action for seduction to which she is a consenting party. Her parent or employer, however, may do so, and is entitled to damages for loss of her service, the seduction in such case being the cause, *"per quod servitiam amisit."*

284. Voluntas, est justa sententia de eo quod quis post mortem suam fieri velit. *A will is an exact opinion or determination concerning that which each one wishes to be done after his death.*

285. Voluntas in delictis, non exitus spectantur. *In criminal cases the intention and not the result is regarded.*

(See Maxs. Nos. 9 and 116.)

286. Vox emissa volat, litera scripta manet. *Word of mouth flies away, things written remain.*

The effect of a written contract cannot be varied in its terms by parol evidence. (See Max. No. 143.)

*** 287. Where one of two innocent parties must suffer by the fraud of another, he who has enabled the fraud to be committed must be the sufferer.**

Thus, if A. on the strength of a representation by B., which is false, signs a receipt, and C., on the faith of the receipt, completes a purchase—here A. must suffer, and not C. (See *French* v. *Hope*, 56 L. J. Ch. 363.)

*** 288. Where there is equal equity the law must prevail.** *That is, who is first in point of time.*

(See Max. No. 220.)

www.ingramcontent.com/pod-product-compliance
Lightning Source LLC
LaVergne TN
LVHW091135180726
843490LV00008B/2989